EUGENE BERMAN

VIEW IN PERSPECTIVE OF A PERFECT SUNSET, 1941

EUGENE BERMAN

Edited and with an Introduction by

Julien Levy

Biography Index Reprint Series

 BOOKS FOR LIBRARIES PRESS

FREEPORT, NEW YORK

First Published 1947

All rights reserved

Reprinted 1971 by arrangement with
Viking Press, Inc.

INTERNATIONAL STANDARD BOOK NUMBER:
0-8369-8078-6

LIBRARY OF CONGRESS CATALOG CARD NUMBER:
73-160915

PRINTED IN THE UNITED STATES OF AMERICA

EUGENE BERMAN

At the time of his earliest exhibition, the painter, Eugene Berman, was called a "neo-romantic." Recently his work has been considered more precisely "neo-baroque." The definitions of both terms are disputable, so let us try to understand their meaning in this particular connection by first outlining their general connotations and then studying in some detail the pictures and life of Berman.

To consider the word "romantic" immediately involves us in mysteries and misapprehensions, this being characteristic of the virtues and also the faults of romantic art — it is out of step with today, any today, and communicates only with yesterdays and tomorrows — it is the dreamer and the seer, memory and prophecy. There is a beauty in the absolutely clear, the innocent and perfectly comprehensible which is called classic, but there has always existed in contrast the beauty which is mysterious, does not tell its whole secret and seems to change with endless and provoking metamorphoses. The former comforts, the latter challenges the eye. The former is lucid, symmetric and in repose whereas the latter, the romantic, is obscure, eccentric, and always in motion, a kind of permanent transition.

We begin to perceive a hint of the relationship between romantic and baroque. Released from the comparative severity of the earlier renaissance by technical mastery of material, the baroque became fluent movement and curves, mystery and surprise, chiaroscuro and illusion. It was related to the past as the flowering of centuries of Western art, but it also bears on problems of our own day. It previewed the spatial relativity of the modern world, the transition from Euclidean geometry to the new calculus, the movement from the still into fragmentation; and a feeling for this kind of motion is Berman's particular gift.

Eugene Berman was born in 1899 in St. Petersburg (Leningrad) into a comfortable professional family of bankers and lawyers. His father died when Berman was seven years old, and his mother remarried. His stepfather, a sympathetic man of good taste, became responsible for the boy's background and education, sending him for schooling to Germany, Switzerland and France, obtaining for him painting instruction with a teacher who was also a practising architect (in the Palladian tradition), and so suggesting the relation of architecture to painting which was to become one of the features of Berman's style.

Waves from the impact of baroque Italy had spread through two hundred years and ten times that in miles, as from a stone dropped in water, losing some original intensity but gathering curious local irregularities, through Spain, France, Germany and Austria to Russia's "Imperial Court City," St. Petersburg. Here the architecture, at farthest separation from its source, was more Eastern, tremendously impressive and flamboyant. This was the city where the boy lived, looked about and sketched, until in 1918 the vicissitudes of the Revolution brought him and his family to Paris and to poverty.

If "putting two and two together" (painting and architecture) had been one of his first important lessons, then taking two and two apart was now Berman's next step in learning the romantic path. Homelessness and separation at a time when he was only nourished by memories and enriched by hope became a recurrent theme in all his subsequent paintings: the *clochards* finding shelter under the arches of the bridges of Paris, the *defaites champêtres* in the park of St. Cloud, beggars on the steps of Italian churches, frugal peasants cultivating the ruins of Les Baux, beachcombers living by the rocks and driftwood in Sicily, lost children of the roads, and the disinherited Indians of the American plains; all somehow environed by the providence of remnants of the past, and all certainly prophetic of displaced persons and the fragmented structure of tomorrow! Out of his brooding sensitive nature, out of the contrasts of his homeless life, out of his defeats and affirmations, appear the inevitable elements for Berman's iconography, his storytelling.

When I first met Berman, he was living in a typical combination of poverty and elegance in an apartment on the *Rue des Lions,* in a building converted from a handsome 18th Century mansion into multiple dwellings, the grand façade and great staircase remaining as a label of taste and dignity (the *Rue des Lions* itself was a converted street, from elegance into slum). The first pictures of his which I saw were of the stables and courtyards of Paris, a period which we might call the period of the "Good Samaritan" as that title was given to

several variations of the courtyard theme. The old tale of the biblical Samaritan provides a good indication to the mood of those paintings: the neighborhood neighborliness lifted parabolically by Berman's interpretation to the level of some contemporary myth.

He had then been living in Paris for a number of years and was beginning to make his mark. His pictures were selling, modestly but steadily, and the critics were mentioning his name with respect as they paid increased attention to the so-called neo-romantic group consisting of Berman, his brother Léonid, and his friends Tchelitchew and Christian Bérard, who had studied with him at the *Academie Ranson*. These young men represented precisely the generation after Picasso (so did the surrealists in another *quartier*) being on an average twenty years younger — unborn at the time when Picasso was painting student pictures, painting student pictures when Picasso consolidated his reputation as a father of new and revolutionary forms. Thus when they, the romantics, arrived at their own age of authority, they were naturally the ones to combine their own action with reaction to "papa." For this reason, it is unlikely that the quality of their leadership can be fully recognized before "papa" is departed.

The romantic group shared sympathetic respect for the "blue" and "rose" periods of Picasso's youth, but they reacted against cubism and the subsequent emphasis on abstraction. They wished to return the human being to the center of the canvas — not the classical nude figure, but costumed emotional man. Therefore they understood such human pictures as Picasso's *Blue Boy*, *Woman Ironing*, or the *Absinthe Drinker* which were all painted in 1905, while they were intolerant to Picasso's cerebral work of 1925 — just twenty years later. This was the year when Berman, Bérard, Léonid, and Tchelitchew presented their first group exhibition at the *Galerie Drouet*. Their pictures then, for the most part, were magnified figure pieces painted in a deliberately limited palette, generally the palette of Picasso's "blue" period. Elements of physiognomy were highly exaggerated, the eyes given particular accent as, romantically considered, eyes might be windows of the soul.* This exhibition at the *Galerie Drouet* was probably the last occasion when the romantic group showed any considerable unanimity of purpose; the temperaments of Bérard and Tchelitchew continuing to pursue the central figure of man, while Berman and Léonid soon shifted their interest to the elaborations of man's environment.**

---

*The surrealists in 1925 were taking a parallel course in reaction to abstract painting, but their interest in individual man was directed to his psychological interior rather than to his exterior projection.

**Léonid's interests led him to specialize in the details of fishing along the coasts of Normandy and Brittany. His fishermen and fisherwomen, while expressively painted, seem no larger than ants against the intricate pattern of oyster beds or the vast expanse of his magnificent seascapes.

They all, of course, took the inevitable *Italienische Reise*, the trip to Italy which Goethe had outlined as a prerequisite to romantic initiation. Berman had first gone in 1922, when he was joined in Venice by Léonid and Bérard. More than the others, he was affected by the architecture. Was it not like St. Petersburg under a different sky? He painted canvases directly from nature, as had young Corot and Courbet, but all these he at once destroyed. "I was discouraged," he explained, "because I wanted to concentrate more things in each picture than my *window* from a single point of view could show." He returned with the others to paint the large figures and portraits of the Drouet exhibition, but through those same years was haunted by the unsolved problems that had unsettled him in Italy. I don't know if he ever read Wordsworth's formula for the romantic, "emotion recollected in tranquility," but he finally decided to sketch from nature and to paint much later from memory. I do know that on a subsequent visit to Italy he met Giorgio de Chirico — another elder painter whose reputation in Paris was by no means so established as that of Picasso. This meeting provided the key which unlocked the doors of Berman's potential. * * *

In an innocent, almost somnambulist way, Chirico had contrived to organize in a single canvas apparently disparate elements of time and space. Such a vigorous hint was enough for Berman and the picture puzzle pieces of his student problems jumped into coherent shape as they were re-animated now by the assurance that the problems *could* be solved. He drew profusely, sketching everything that interested his eye without worrying how, where, or when they would combine into a definitive painting. He felt much less unease in making a transition from façade to interior (by simply walking through the door) or from landscape to cityscape, from nature to museums and back again. Thus he could acquaint himself at once with the way a certain Luigi stacked his rowboats at night on a Neapolitan beach and covered them with tarpaulin and with the way Piranese stacked his incredible arches of cross-hatched lines.

Armed with plenty of sketches, he returned to Paris and in the studio painted his particular combination of transmuted memories. He retained the sombre blue palette which seemed appropriate to pictures that had become half nocturnal reveries. Later he was to attack the problem of moving more easily from night to day, and back again. At this moment the nocturnal style was so fitting that it was to continue until its impetus was exhausted naturally (Plates I and II). And he wandered through the streets of Paris, along the *Rue de Vaugirard* or *Rue de la Convention* and other magical streets, again applying the same technique of sketching reality, but painting later from memory and from dream. The results were the series of neighborhood Parisian courtyards

*** The surrealists also found in Chirico's metaphysical paintings an important source of inspiration. The extent of Chirico's influence is described in James Thrall Soby's book, *The Early Chirico*.

VII

and stables we have called the period of the "Good Samaritan," the material, as we have already noted, for his first success as a matured artist (Plates III, IV and VI).

At this moment light, that was not moonlight, crept into his palette. Doors opened off the courtyard and permitted a rosy glow of lamplight to dissipate the heavy nocturnal blue. They also allowed occasional glimpses of interiors humbly illumined by that special, warm, rosy lamp or candlelight that the French painter, Georges de la Tour, had understood more intimately than any Italian master of chiaroscuro. While Tchelitchew had started to experiment intellectually with the balance between contrasting blues and reds, "hot and cold colors," and Bérard with, "the opposition of poison colors," Berman arrived at an expedient alternation by simply walking in and out of these open doors. A series of nocturnal interiors was the result, and finally an interior in brighter key — *Dawn* (Plate IX). Here, through the door, daylight is visible.

With all this sketching to be done right around the corner it should not be thought that Berman was ever to lose his close and studious intercourse with the past. During this period he spent a great amount of time exploring museums and libraries. In the Louvre he found Jacopo Bellini's book of drawings, *Le Receuil Valardi*, with its Venetian processionals which fascinated him, and from that starting point could trace the development of the liberal drawing technique culminating in the superb performances of Tiepolo. Temperamentally, Berman could not, and should not, draw with the continuous classic line of Fouquet or Ingres. His caligraphy was becoming passionate and broken, while always retaining a complete legibility. A nervous line, never fully defining a form which must change from second to second into motion and new outline, always incomplete, always promising, thereby at once mysterious and inevitable — such line when combined with flourishes of wash modelling is the essence of great baroque drawing which, in schoolman vocabulary, is termed "virtuoso." This particular and difficult style Berman mastered.

In the libraries too, there were bound to be books reminding him of his beloved Italian architecture: early editions of Serlio, plans and façades of the buildings designed by Bramante, Scamozzi, Alberti, St. Gallo, Baldassare Peruzzi (to mention some of Berman's favorites). He wanted so much to revisit Venice, to see Palladio's Olympic Theatre in Vicenza and to paint the Prato della Valle in Padua. In the summer of 1931 he again had the opportunity and he went.

This year he relaxed more fully to daylight and the flamboyant style — in his own words, he was "tempted by the fluent exhuberance of baroque." Not only had he extended his palette, but the texture of his material and compositional structure were changing. One of the up-to-date aspects common to all the neo-romantic painters was a persistent interest in fundamental mechanics of the painter's craft. They each had tried out various new media, such as pigments mixed with sand, Duco, wax, or even coffee grounds mixed with roofer's paint. Berman's particular contribution to these experiments was mothered by necessity: he could not afford many fine new canvases and the quantity of pigment needed to build the desired impasto of heavy underpainting, so he bought valueless old paintings at the Flea Market, repaired the canvases and primed them. This produced a good resilient surface; in addition, the texture of the earlier paint roughened the surface with lumps, lines, and ambiguous configurations which furnished provocative counterpoint to the shapes and perspectives of Berman's own composition, and faced him with the enigma which continued to preoccupy him in later years, namely the conflict of the two dimensional picture plane against the painted illusion of a third dimension.

His approach to perspective at this time was elaborated with considerable vigour. His pictures were no longer to be entered on the central axis while distances receded in measured cubes like a nest of boxes. This kind of organization had been a solution when Berman was trying to combine representational images with the architectonics of Picasso's cubism. The series of "Nocturnes" and "Good Samaritan" pictures would have looked almost as if they were abstractions had they not been so evidently arrangements of recognizable courts, walls, and windows. Now his design was to become complicated by ogee curves and off-center dynamic equilibrium.

In the new explosive compositions of Paduan vistas and Venetian piazzas (Plates XIV, XV and XXII), Berman's frozen somnolent humans are contrasted with a series of mutilated statues so vividly animated that they seem on the point of stepping from their pedestals to resume life that depleted humanity has abandoned. Marble is frantically anxious to continue the march of civilization: the pavement draws circles around discouraged people, bridges leap their span like optimistic ponies while noble statues wrestle against their time-corroded petrifaction with all the hopeful agony of Laocoön.

In France this series of statues, the struggle of the Marble Age, continues in the elegant parks of Versailles and St. Cloud. Perhaps in France Berman became aware of a more rational pessimism: the statues seem mournful too, but the element of landscape is new and lively under the influence of Poussin, Courbet, and Corot

(Plates XVIII, XXVII and XXVIII). If both statue and flesh seem more discouraged, foliage and clouds have become articulate. Not merely articulate but almost demoniacal by the following year when Berman went to Les Baux. This is a hidden place near Arles, built into the cliffs which surround a plateau and dominate a fantastic landscape, where the mistral regularly drives people out of their minds, and a band of penniless peasants try miserably to cultivate a soil that is clogged by the ruins of an ancient fortress town and the weird shapes of chalk rock formations (Plates XXIX, XXX, and XXXI).* Berman's dreams were turning into nightmares — perhaps it was time to pack up and move on.

Berman's work had earned him an appreciative public in America. His friends in New York were urging his visit. After a short interim of hesitation, he made his first journey to New York in 1935 and eventually became an American citizen.

In America the whole scale of his work underwent a dramatic change. He began by executing a series of magnificent mural decorations, first for my own apartment, then panels for the dining room of James Thrall Soby's house in Connecticut, and later for Wright Ludington in California and John Yeon in Oregon. He also designed a setting for the concert stage of the Hartford museum,** *Matinée Musicale*, and an entrance of costumes in the Paper Ball during the Hartford Music Festival of 1936,*** revealing a longtime preoccupation with theatre which was to result in the designing of costumes and settings for several matchless ballet productions (illustrated at the end of the book). His style in these various media made an impression on American fashion, as his influence was circulated by publications, beginning with "Town & Country" magazine which ran a handsome cover design by Berman in 1937.

This sudden profusion in all except the expected direction can perhaps be attributed to the abrupt change-over from the Old to the New World. It certainly was not accomplished in hope for greater remuneration, as he was succeeding more surely with his smaller pictures. It must have resulted from an uncontrollable urge to expand, in this novel vacuum of the Western Hemisphere, the accumulated pressure of his creative occupation, to unpack as it were the furnishings of his imagination and symbolically relieve the acute homelessness which had formed his background. For the purpose of executing his commission on the Ludington murals he

---

*Sometimes called "Val d'Enfer," which Dante was supposed to have visited during his exile in Provence.
** Wadsworth Atheneum & Morgan Memorial, Hartford, Conn.
*** Berman's entrance was called "Les Ruines d'Hartford: 3036."

went to California, traversing the awesome and seemingly endless deserts of Arizona and New Mexico (Plates LX and LXI). In retrospect his busy imagination overran those barren "wide open spaces" with projects for architecture of a grandeur seldom seen before — Bermanesque arches and monuments, avenues and vistas, that would conquer the interminable horizon and tame the inhumanity of space (Plates LXII and LXIII). The fact that these vast rural reconstruction jobs were half in ruins even while they were in process of building would not prove untypical of either Berman or America.

A central figure in some of these impressive compositions is the figure of a woman, her head bowed and her hair mournfully shrouding her face. In her attitude she resembles the mysterious *Derelitta* of Botticelli, but instead of sitting against a closed door as in Botticelli's picture, the door is open, or unfinished, or simply not there — and great distances stretch behind her. In later arrangements we find her standing with her back towards the spectator, looking into the canvas and towards the horizon (Plates LXIV and LXVIII). Just how much of despair and how much of hope there is in this figure is hard to ascertain. She seems somehow unresolved, waiting. Very soon she fills the whole picture frame, playing the heroine of a modern mythology in high tragic vein (Plates LXXIII, LXXIV, LXXVIII and LXXXV). *Proserpina* when she is in the dark and waiting for the light, *Muse of the Western World* when she is most glamorous, *Andromeda* abandoned and enchained, ****Cassandra* as she faces the burning of her world.

Beside the poetic content that is always present in Berman's work, we must recognize that each period represents, as it should to any sincere craftsman, a new technical problem that has been mastered. We have followed Berman's progress from monochrome to an extended palette, from severe to complex composition, from architectural rendering to atmospheric landscape, from easel dimension to theatre dimension, and now the attitudes, psychology, and costuming of large figure pieces are achieved. The painting of *Proserpina II* (Plate XCVIII) marks the culmination of this series. It also introduces a complicating factor — the manner by which the surface of the canvas is invaded by deliberate spots, tears, and painted holes, forming an elaborate network of artificial patina. To understand this development properly we must retrace our steps almost to the beginning of Berman's career. The cycle is nearly complete.

In the early days when Berman was buying his canvases at the Flea Market, we remarked that there appeared a problem of counterpoint between the surface texture and the spatial illusion. Other preoccupations interrupted further elaboration of this motif until it was resumed in the first American murals. The panels for my apartment were executed in detailed *trompe l'oeil* (Plates XXXIX and XL). The apparently inlaid wood frames were not wood but a meticulously painted simulation, with nail holes, worm holes, and cast shadows painted to give a convincing relief. The background was a solid color and the walls of the room were to match that color so that the deception of an "empty" frame was convincing and there was no indication as to where the walls ended and the Berman painting began. The Soby murals (Plates XXXV, XXXVI, XXXVII and XXXVIII) were more formal, as a surge of memories from a recent voyage to Sicily provoked a masterly restatement of Sicilian themes, a chorus of mobile transfigurations of the beachcombers and debris; but the Ludington murals again approached the problem of "where is the wall?" by the false-torn surfaces and apparently tacked-on sketches which seemed to be peeling off the wall and into the room almost further than the purposefully shallow perspective carried back (Plates LI and LII). An additional series of sketches at this time formed a project which unfortunately was never carried out. In these the walls would have been shown as openings with the landscape painted in deep perspective through the illusory arches, giving the picturesque illusion of a dramatically enlarged room (Plate LVIII).

The deceptive placing, the ambiguous figures, and the shrapnel punctured architecture of the canvases during the years of World War II (Plates XC to XCVIII) continue to stir up in our imagination doubts, solutions, and then new doubts again, about space and time and their relation. In describing the later pictures of Berman, I have used the word "counterpoint" with a conscious, irresistible reference to music. Music has a secret that it is able to whisper to the ear alone, (the ear and the eye are physically very separate) and that secret is that time, which is the musical medium, is modified by melodic line, harmonic depth, and orchestral coloring. But line, depth, and coloring are essentials of the painter's craft, and have to do with space! Berman subjects his knowledge of space to new time-space considerations, and has engaged his notations to suggestive musical connotations.

We see that the periphery of Berman's production is expanding in profuse variations, while his grave center remains strongly anchored — because he is not inconstant, because he is a painter of stubborn courage, his arduous progress has won for him both perspective and momentum. The baroque-to-modern arc of his talent is clear, and its spiral trajectory is the most promising sign of significant creation.

**** Notice that the "shackles" of *Andromeda* (Plate LXXVIII) are not really binding — she is tied more by her own imagination and inhibitions.

XI

Supplement

The following was written on the occasion of a visit with Eugene Berman in the autumn of 1946. The painter was unusually articulate, discussing his ideas of painting in general and of his own in particular. Without any attempt at continuity or completeness, I offer my impressions of some of his views.

Berman thinks that art is "timeless." To be classified as of the present day is alien to him — today being only the brief link between the great past and a limitless future. As a man of "his time," he is permitted to react against it as well as to move with it, to walk the alleys of memory or to contemplate paths of the future. Our thoughts and sensations are made of innumerable meanderings in every direction and domain. In the 20th Century, the most primitive man cannot conserve a completely simple mind untouched by knowledge of present and past civilizations.

As one can explore time back and forth with complete familiarity and the consciousness of parallels between sensations and thoughts centuries apart, the aspects, form and colors of diverse things can merge, interpenetrate, and create double, triple, multiple images and infinite visual associations and transformations. A model posing for Berman is only interesting if she suggests some creature out of mythology — heroine, muse, sybil or goddess. Clouds can become mountains or underseascapes, expressive draperies mold the form of bodies that are not there, and cascades of dangling hair express more drama than the face which is hidden beneath. Holes painted into the surface of the canvas not only simulate decay or destruction, but also act as a two-dimensional counterpoint to the third dimension of illusionist perspective. Berman admires illusionist representation of things because, in order to be convincing and fully comprehensible to the spectator, unreality must seem one hundred percent real.

Nevertheless, it should not be thought that Berman's work avoids reality because it is poetic or fantastic. Again it is a matter of merging the inner and the outer eye. Part of his inspiration is always derived from real things and real people — or from a photo, a newspaper clipping, an architectural blueprint, a ruined building, someone else's painting, a natural landscape, or a pebble on the beach. All these are part of his vocabulary, everything from Nature including that part of Nature that is made by Man.

His mediation amidst diverse influences may be called "eclectic," but only in the sense that the Renaissance, Berman's favorite period, was particularly eclectic. At that time, the artist was not only an accomplished specialist in his own craft but also skillful in almost every other craft. Berman's devotion to the theatre and architecture is a nostalgic symptom of his regret that in another age he might have been encouraged as a builder, goldsmith, sculptor, and inventor, with no loss to his abilities as a painter because each function is an outgrowth and complement of another, interchangeable links, indestructible but embracing everything — every domain, every art and craft and spiritual manifestation.

Berman believes that a serious problem of our modern age is the schism between universal and specialized man. Each has his qualities and each his faults, but the function of both should be reconciled with each other. The division between creative artists is represented by the revolutionary who breaks with the sense of the past to pioneer new discoveries, and by that other, whatever name we call him, who wishes to keep the universal circle complete, to contribute himself to the sum of all previous efforts, ideas, and ideals.

JULIEN LEVY

INDEX

TITLE	DATE	COLLECTION	PLATE
The Adriatic	1932	James Thrall Soby, Farmington	XXIII
Andromeda	1943		LXXVIII
The Antique Column (Trompe L'Oeil)	1936	Edward James, Hollywood	XLI
Apollo and Daphne	1933	James Thrall Soby, Farmington	XXVIII
Ariadne in Oregon	1942	Kenneth MacPherson, New York	LXVIII
At the Gates of the Town (Nightfall)	1937	James Thrall Soby, Farmington	XLIV
Ballet Settings	1932-46		Pages 64-79
The Bridge	1930	Julien Green, Paris	II
The Bridges of Paris	1932	Philadelphia Museum of Fine Arts	XXVI
The Broken Crock	1938		XLVIII
Cassandra	1942-43		LXXIV
The Chariot	1930	James Thrall Soby, Farmington	V
The Church of St. Guistina	1931	Agnes Rindge, Poughkeepsie	XVI
The Concert	1942	Arthur Sachs, Santa Barbara	LXVI
Conversation Piece in Monument Valley	1941		LXI
Cover Designs	1940-45		Page 80
Dark Muse	1944		LXXXIII
Daughters of Fire	1942		LXXV
Dawn	1931	Phillips Memorial Gallery, Washington	IX
Death in Venice	1945-46	John Yeon, Portland	XCII
Debris on the Beach	1934	Agnes Rindge, Poughkeepsie	XXXII
Desolate Landscape	1936	Julien Levy, New York	XXXIV
Dining Room with Mural Panels	1936	James Thrall Soby, Farmington	XXXV to XXXVIII
Divertissements			XCIX to CI
Drawings	1944		LXXXVI
		Darius Milhaud, Paris	LXXXVII
		John Goodwin	LXXXVIII
			LXXXIX
Flight into Egypt	1941	Frederick Stettenheim, New York	LXII
The Good Samaritan (Study)	1930	Museum of Modern Art, New York	III
The Good Samaritan (Study)	1930	Museum of Modern Art, New York	VI
The Good Samaritan (Variation)	1930	Washington University, St. Louis	IV
Imaginary Portrait of Isabella d'Este in her Studio	1945-46	C. Iolas, New York	XCVII
Imaginary View of Rome in the Time of Lorenzo Bernini	1939	Luther Greene	LVII
Live Still Life	1942-43		LXX
Lorelei in Oregon	1940-41		LXIV
Lost Children of the Roads	1938		LIII
The Lovers	1931	Agnes Rindge, Poughkeepsie	XI
The Magic Circle, Venice	1932	Ruth Page Fisher, Chicago	XXII
Medusa's Corner	1943		LXXVII
Melancholy	1936	George Lauder Greenway, New York	XLII
Melancholy (Water color)	1943		LXXVI
Memories of Ischia	1931	James Thrall Soby, Farmington	X
Memories of St. Cloud	1932	Mr. & Mrs. Henry Clifford, Radnor	XXI
Memories of Verona	1931	Thomas F. Howard, New York	XII
Memory of Chioggia	1932	Mr. & Mrs. R. Kirk Askew, Jr., New York	XVII
Memory of Venice (Study)	1932	James Thrall Soby, Farmington	XIX
Miserere	1945		XCV
Mural Decoration	1938	Wright Ludington, Santa Barbara	LI, LII
The Muse of the Western World	1942	Metropolitan Museum of Art, New York	LXXIII

The Mutilated Statue	1933	Julien Levy, New York	XXVII
The Natural Bridge	1933	Kenneth MacPherson, New York	XXIX
Nature Très Morte	1945	Mrs. Huttleston Rogers, New York	XCI
Nightfall	1937	Arthur Jeffres, London	XLV
Night Music (Imaginary Portrait of Ona Munson)	1942	Jere Abbott, Northampton	LXVII
Night Music (Water color)	1942	Jere Abbott, Northampton	LXV
Niké	1943		LXXI
Niké (Sketch)	1943		LXXII
Offering to the Night	1938	Mrs. Kenyon Boocock	LIV
Paludia	1938		XLVII
Park of St. Cloud	1932	Vassar College Museum, Poughkeepsie	XVIII
Portrait of Rico Lebrun	1945		XC
Project for a Mural	1940		LVIII
Proserpina	1944		LXXXV
Proserpina (Drawing)	1944		LXXXIV
Proserpina II	1945-46		XCVIII
Provence-Les Baux	1933	James Thrall Soby, Farmington	XXXI
The Pyramid	1932		XXIV
Red Nets	1935	Henry Clifford, Radnor	XXXIII
Restless Landscape	1933	John Yeon, Portland	XXX
The Rialto	1931	Julien Levy, New York	XIII
Sea Port with Sails	1928	Wadsworth Atheneum, Hartford	I
Sentinels of the Night	1938		LV
Siciliana	1937	Henry Clifford, Radnor	XLIII
The Silent Dance	1944		LXXX
The Silent Dance (Variation Study)	1944		LXXIX
Sleeping Youth	1932	Museum of Fine Arts, Boston	XXV
The Sleep of Stone	1938		XLIX
Soledad	1942		LXIX
The Spring	1945-46		XCVI
The Stable	1930		VII
Stage (See Ballet Settings)			
Star Ridden Night	1945	Geoffrey Gilmour	XCIV
Statue and Its Shadow	1931	Sociètè des Amies des Artistes Vivantes	XV
Statues in a Park (Study)	1932	James Thrall Soby, Farmington	XX
Storm over Cefalu	1937		XLVI
Sunset-Medusa	1945		XCIII
Time and the Monuments	1941	John Yeon, Portland	LXIII
Tobias and the Angel	1938	Charles P. Cooley, Hartford	L
To the Glory of the Setting Sun	1941		LX
Trompe L'Oeil Panels	1936		XXXIX, XL
Unfinished Music	1944		LXXXII
Unfinished Music (Study)	1944		LXXXI
View in Perspective of a Perfect Sunset	1941	Henry Clifford, Radnor	
View of Prato Della Valle	1931	Mrs. F. S. Goodwin, Hartford	XIV
Villa Adriana at Tivoli	1931		VIII
Wash Drawing	1939		LVI
Wash Drawing	1939		LIX

Acknowledgment is given to the Julien Levy Gallery for the photographs of the paintings and drawings, to the Museum of Modern Art and Dance Index for the photographs of the "Romeo and Juliet" costume designs. Paintings with no collection listed are either in the collection of the artist or Julien Levy Gallery.

PLATE I   Sea Port with Sails, 1928

PLATE II   The Bridge, 1930

PLATE III   The Good Samaritan (Study), 1930   PLATE IV   The Good Samaritan (Variation), 1930

PLATE V   The Chariot, 1930   PLATE VI   The Good Samaritan (Study), 1930

PLATE VII   The Stable, 1930

PLATE VIII

Villa Adriana at Tivoli, 1931

PLATE IX   Dawn, 1931

4

PLATE X   Memories of Ischia, 1931

PLATE XI   The Lovers, 1931

PLATE XIII   The Rialto, 1931

PLATE XIV

View of Prato Della Valle, 1931

PLATE XII (opposite)

Memories of Verona, 1931

8

PLATE XVI   The Church of St. Guistina, 1931

PLATE XVII   Memory of Chioggia, 1932

PLATE XV (opposite)

Statue and Its Shadow, 1931

PLATE XIX   Memory of Venice (Study), 1932

PLATE XXI (Below)   Memories of St. Cloud, 1932

PLATE XVIII   Park of St. Cloud, 1932

PLATE XX   Statues in a Park (Study), 1932

PLATE XXII   The Magic Circle, Venice, 1932

PLATE XXIII The Adriatic, 1932

PLATE XXIV The Pyramid, 1932

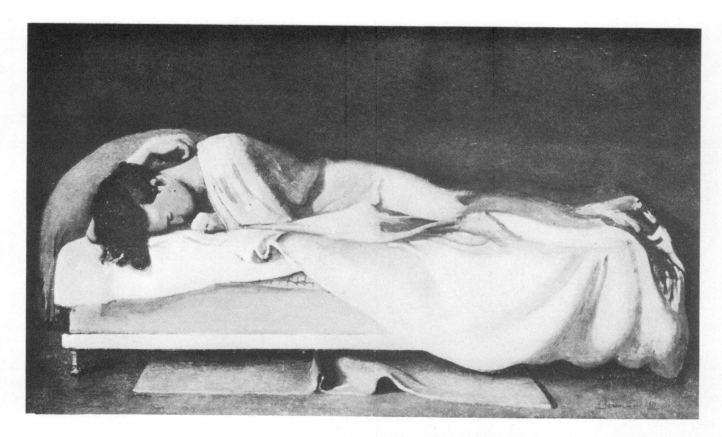

PLATE XXV   Sleeping Youth, 1932

PLATE XXVI   The Bridges of Paris, 1932

PLATE XXVII   The Mutilated Statue, 1933

PLATE XXVIII   Apollo and Daphne, 1933

14

PLATE XXIX   The Natural Bridge, 1933

PLATE XXX   Restless Landscape, 1933

15

PLATE XXXI   Provence—Les Baux, 1933

PLATE XXXII
    Debris on the Beach, 1934

PLATE XXXIII   Red Nets, 1935

PLATE XXXIV   Desolate Landscape, 1936

17

PLATES XXXV to XXXVIII   Dining Room with Mural Panels in the Residence of James Thrall Soby, 1936

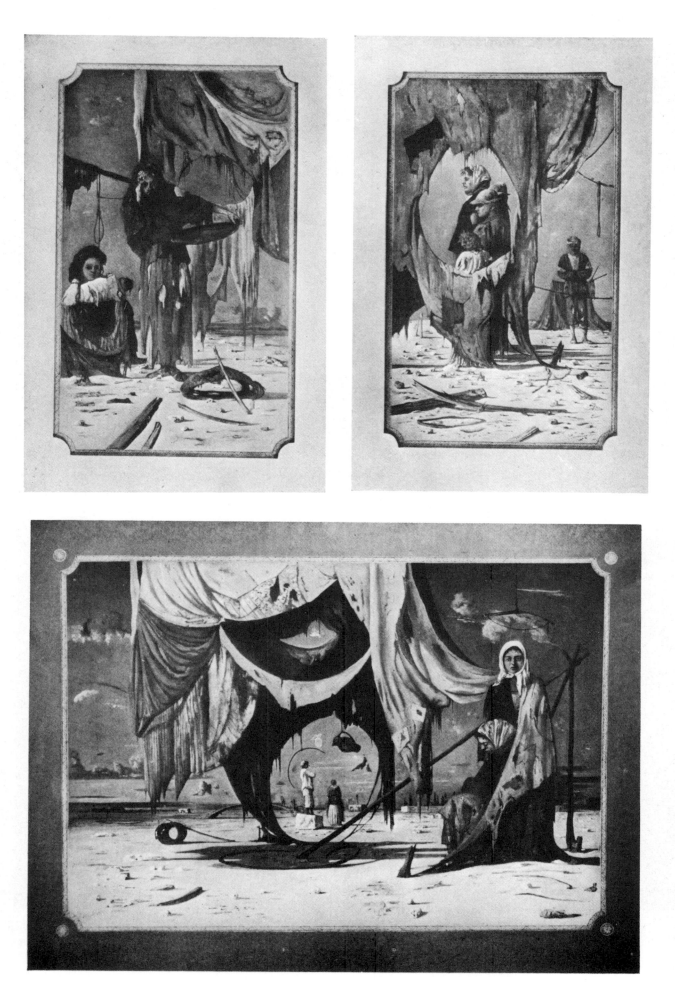

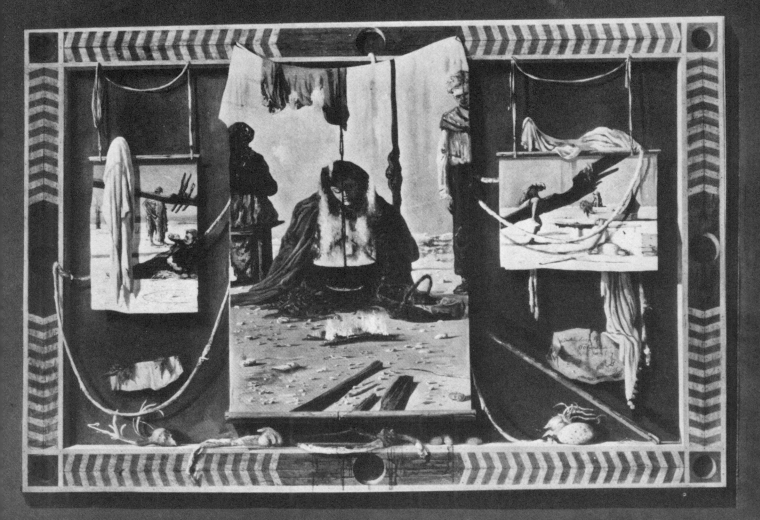

PLATES XXXIX and XL

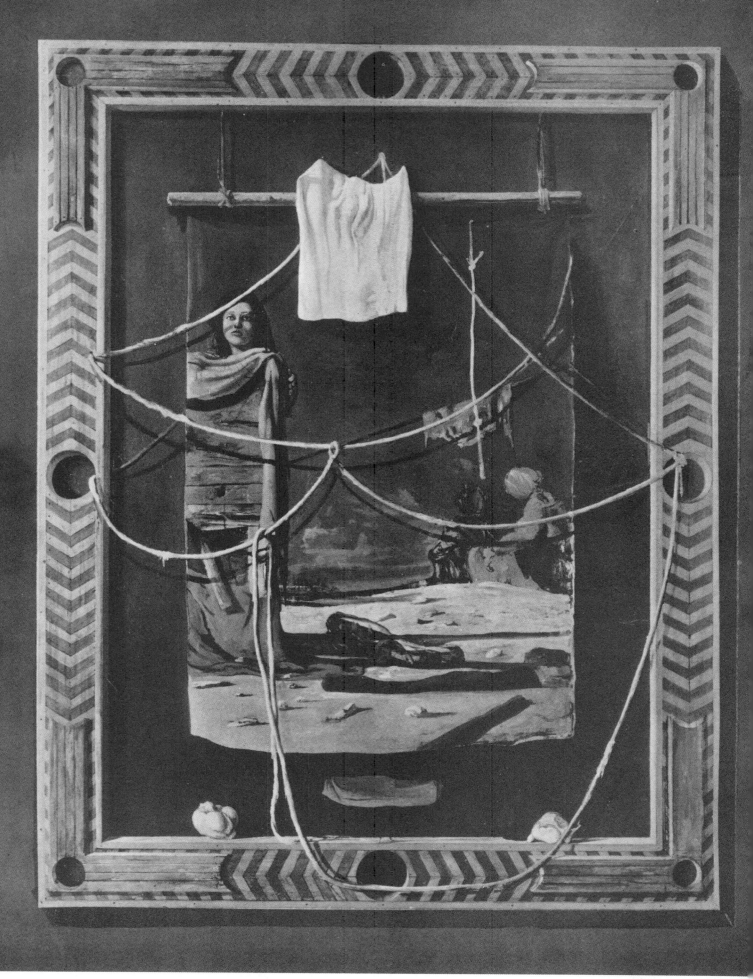

Trompe L'Oeil Panels for a Mural Decoration, 1936

PLATE XLI

The Antique Column (Trompe L'Oeil), 1936

22

PLATE XLII   Melancholy, 1936

PLATE XLIII   Siciliana, 1937

PLATE XLIV   At the Gates of the Town (Nightfall), 1937   PLATE XLV   Nightfall, 1937

PLATE XLVI   Storm over Cefalu, 1937   PLATE XLVII   Paludia, 1938

PLATE XLVIII   The Broken Crock, 1938   PLATE XLIX   The Sleep of Stone, 1938

PLATE L   Tobias and the Angel, 1938

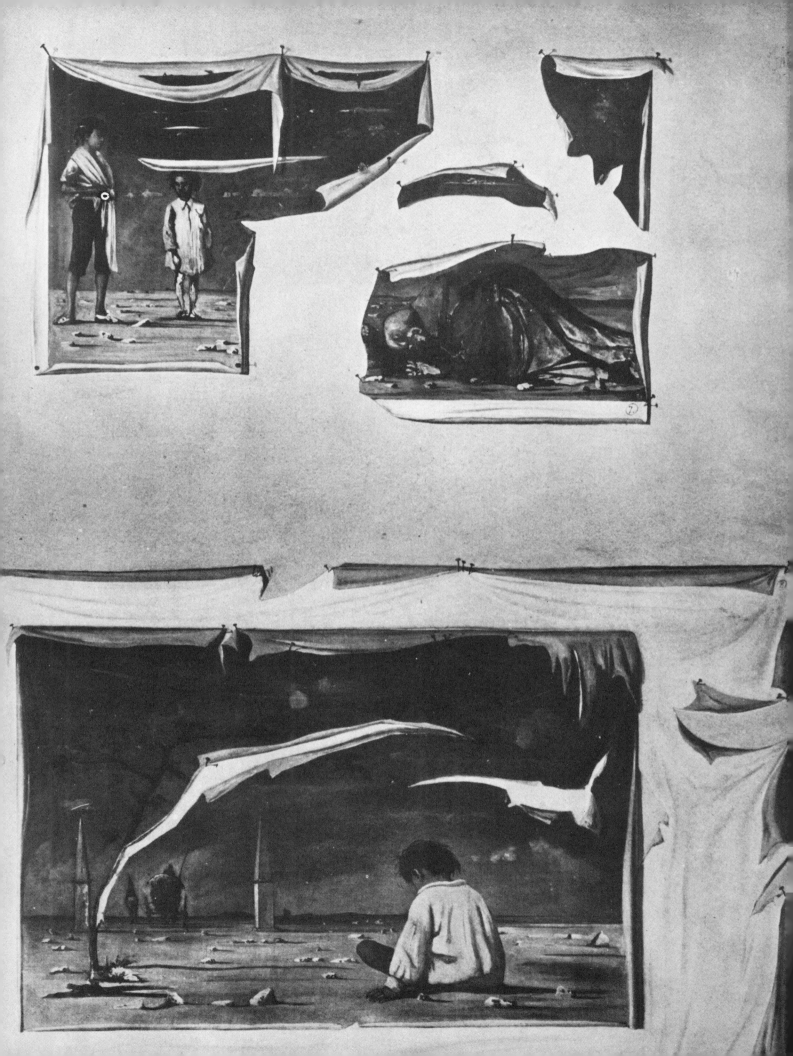

PLATES LI and LII

Mural Decoration for the Residence of Wright Ludington, 1938

PLATE LIII   Lost Children of the Roads, 1938

PLATE LIV   Offering to the Night, 1938

30

PLATE LV

Sentinels of the Night, 1938

PLATE LVI

Wash Drawing, 1939

PLATE LVII

Imaginary View of Rome in the Time of Lorenzo Bernini, 1939

PLATE LVIII　　　　　　Project for a Mural, 1940

PLATE LIX　　　　　　Wash Drawing, 1939

33

PLATE LX To the Glory of the Setting Sun, 1941   PLATE LXI Conversation Piece in Monument Valley, 1941

PLATE LXII

Flight into Egypt, 1941

PLATE LXIII   Time and the Monuments, 1941

PLATE LXIV   Lorelei in Oregon, 1940-41

PLATE LXV   Night Music (Water color), 1942

PLATE LXVI   The Concert, 1942

PLATE LXVII   Night Music (Imaginary Portrait of Ona Munson), 1942

PLATE LXVIII   Ariadne in Oregon, 1942

PLATE LXIX   Soledad, 1942

PLATE LXX (opposite)   Live Still Life, 1942-43

40

PLATE LXXI   Niké, 1943

PLATE LXXII   Niké (Sketch), 1943

42

PLATE LXXIII
The Muse of the Western World, 1942

PLATE LXXIV   Cassandra, 1942-43

44

PLATE LXXV

Daughters of Fire, 1942

46

PLATE LXXVII   Medusa's Corner, 1943

PLATE LXXVI (opposite)   Melancholy (Water color), 1943

47

PLATE LXXVIII   Andromeda, 1943

PLATE LXXIX

The Silent Dance (Variation Study), 1944

48

PLATE LXXX

The Silent Dance, 1944

49

PLATE LXXXI   Unfinished Music (Study), 1944

PLATE LXXXII   Unfinished Music, 1944

PLATE LXXXIII

Dark Muse, 1944

PLATE LXXXIV   Proserpina (Drawing), 1944

52

PLATE LXXXV

Proserpina, 194

PLATES LXXXVI and LXXXVII

Drawings, 1944

PLATES LXXXVIII and LXXXIX
Drawings, 1944

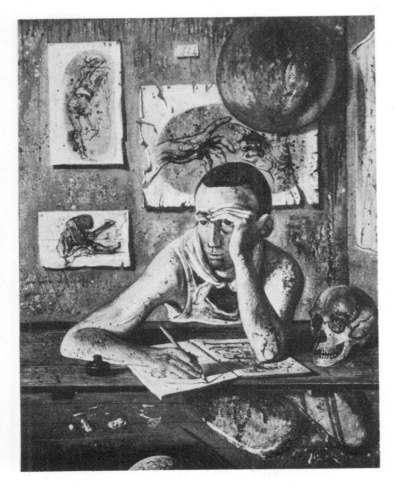

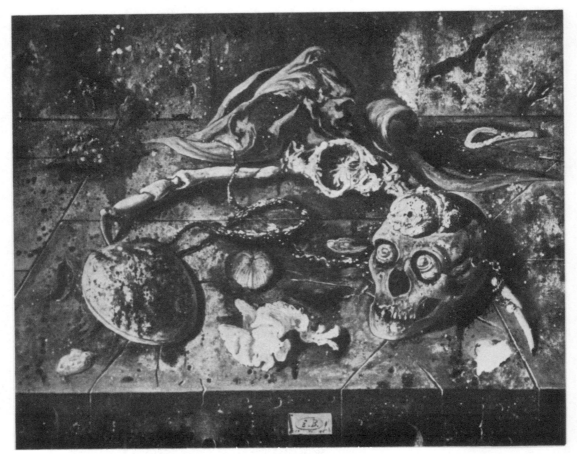

56

PLATE XCII   Death in Venice, 1945-46

PLATE XCIII   Sunset-Medusa, 1945

PLATE XCIV   Star Ridden Night, 1945

PLATE XCV

PLATE XCVI   The Spring, 1945-46

PLATE XCVII

    Imaginary Portrait of Isabella d'Este
in her Studio, 1945-46

PLATE XCVIII

Proserpina II, 1945-46

DIVERTISSEMENTS

PLATES XCIX to CI

BALLET
SETTINGS

VENETIAN SETTING
(Experimental Stage Model), 1932

Photograph: Courtesy Wadsworth Atheneum

ITALIAN SCENE
(Experimental Stage Model), 1932

Costume for
ICARE
(Ballet Russe de Monte Carlo), 1935

Costume for
ICARE
(Ballet Russe de Monte Carlo), 1938

Photograph: Courtesy Museum of Modern Art

Italian Symphony
(Project), 1939

Italian Symphony
(Project), 1939

Settings and Costumes for

DEVIL'S HOLIDAY

(Ballet Russe de Monte Carlo), 1939

Settings and Costumes for

CONCERTO BAROCCO

(American Ballet Caravan), 1941

Model Settings for THE ISLAND GOD, 1942

Costumes and Settings for

ROMEO AND JULIET

(Ballet Theatre), 1943

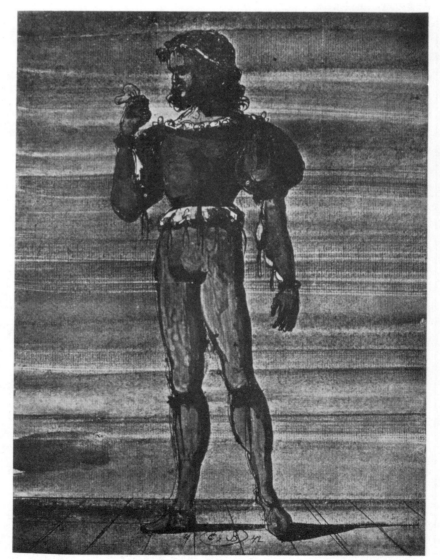

ROMEO AND JULIET (Continued)

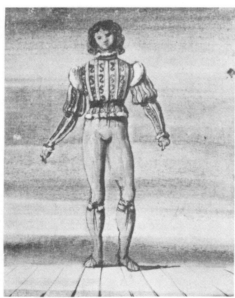

Photographs: Courtesy Museum of Modern Art

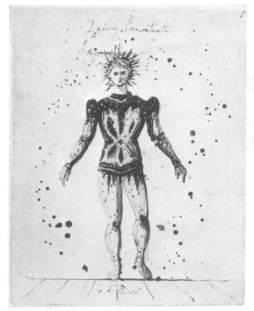

Costumes for DANSES CONCERTANTES

(Ballet Russe de Monte Carlo), 1944

DÉCOR TRAGIQUE, 1935–1944

BOURGEOIS GENTILHOMME
(Two Variations for the Curtain)
Ballet Russe de Monte Carlo, 1944

Settings for GISELLE (Ballet Theatre), 1946

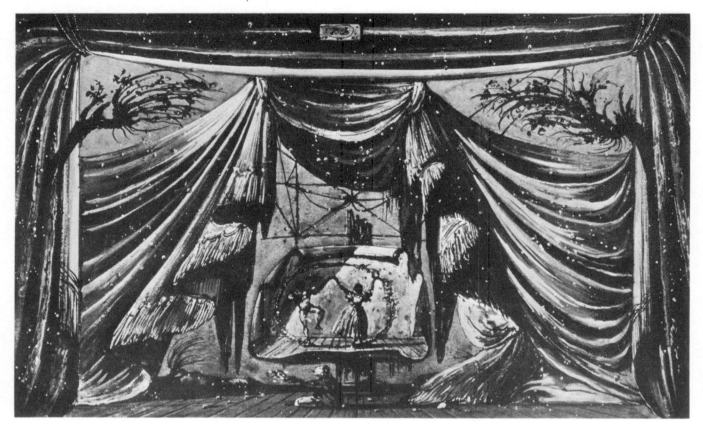

Above: Curtain for Act I

Below: Project for Act I

GISELLE (Continued)

Above: Model for Act II

76

GISELLE (Continued)   Below: Project for Act II

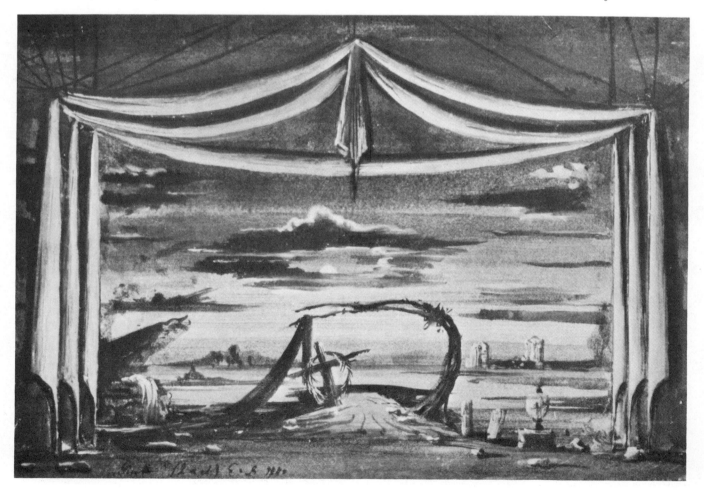

GISELLE (Continued)

Settings and Costumes for   ARMIDA   (Imaginary Ballet), 1946

(*Richard Davis Collection*)

(*Courtesy of the Publishers*)